CONTEMPORARY IS...   ...Y

C000145404

This book is due for return on or before the last date shown below.

Ur

OXFORD UNIVERSITY PRESS

ACKNOWLEDGEMENTS

The publishers and author would like to thank the following person for her permission to use copyright material:

p.25 Melanie Friend, Hutchinson Library.

All other photographs are supplied by the author.

The cover photograph is reproduced by permission of Raghu Rai, Magnum Photos.

Illustrations are by Herb Bowes Graphics, Oxford.

Every effort has been made to trace and contact copyright holders, but this has not always been possible. We apologise for any infringement of copyright.

Thanks are due to Virginia, who read and commented so constructively on the draft text.

Oxford University Press, Walton Street, Oxford OX2 6DP.

Oxford New York Toronto Delhi Bombay Calcutta Madras Karachi Petaling Jaya Singapore Hong Kong Tokyo Nairobi Dar es Salaam Cape Town Melbourne Auckland
and associated companies in
Berlin Ibadan

Oxford is a trade mark of Oxford University Press

© Oxford University Press 1992

ISBN 0 19 913370 0

Typeset by Gem Publishing Company, Wallingford
Design and artwork by Herb Bowes Graphics, Oxford
Printed by M & A Thomson Litho Ltd, East Kilbride, Scotland

PREFACE

Contemporary Issues in Geography is a series of books dealing with issues of concern in today's society. The series was developed as a result of our own teaching needs, especially when preparing INSET courses for teachers in Coventry and Warwickshire.

Hugh Matthews and Ian Foster, Series Editors

This book

By the close of the present century, for every person found living in a town or city in a developed country, two will be residing in a Third World city. Until quite recently, urban settlements were seen as signs of a modern way of life and of development. But current Third World cities are urbanising far more rapidly than those of the industrialised world in their heyday. Today's Third World cities are associated with low levels of industrialisation, marked inequalities between regions, and massive problems of housing and employment provision. This book aims to introduce readers to the debates concerning the role that cities play in the process of Third World development, a key issue in contemporary world geography.

Rob Potter

CONTENTS

Forty slum children
die in mud avalanche

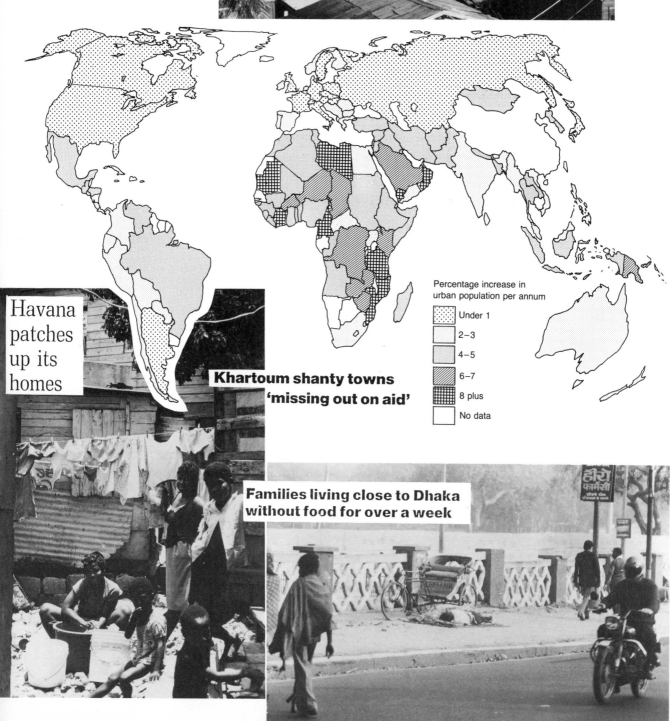

Havana
patches
up its
homes

**Khartoum shanty towns
'missing out on aid'**

**Families living close to Dhaka
without food for over a week**

Percentage increase in
urban population per annum

Under 1

2–3

4–5

6–7

8 plus

No data

Part I

THIRD WORLD CITIES AND ISSUES OF DEVELOPMENT

1 THE URBAN EXPLOSION IN THE THIRD WORLD

1.1 Introduction

Urbanisation is one of the most significant processes affecting human societies in the twentieth century. Until recent times, urbanisation was regarded as a direct sign of modernisation and development. Throughout history, industrialisation and urbanisation have tended to occur together. But this relationship, one which has held for more than 6000 years since the emergence of the first cities, has changed fundamentally since 1945.

We are currently experiencing an entirely new era of world urbanisation, and this is resulting in the need for politicians and planners to reinterpret the role that cities play in the processes of social and economic development. This book focuses on the important issues which surround this highly topical debate.

Today, it is the countries making up the Third World that are experiencing the highest rates of urbanisation. Figure 1.1 gives a clear indication of this. The simple association which previously held between cities, industry and modernisation has been broken. Towns and cities in the Third World are growing much more quickly than cities like London, Paris and New York did during and after the Industrial Revolution in the eighteenth and nineteenth centuries. This is giving rise to an *urban explosion* in the Third World.

◀ *Figure 1.1 Urbanisation is occurring rapidly in the Third World and it is now recognised that the urban poor are doing their best to help themselves under very difficult conditions. The map shows the rates of urbanisation for the countries of the world in 1986. The photos show scenes from Third World cities and the newspaper headlines indicate how these cities make the news*

1.2 Urbanisation, urban growth, and urbanism in the Third World

There are three processes involved in this urban explosion:

(i)   The first is leading an increasing proportion of the total population of regions and nations to live in places defined as urban. This process of *relative* concentration is referred to as *urbanisation*.

(ii) This should not be confused with *urban growth*, which is the *absolute* increase in the physical size and total population of urban areas.

(iii) Finally, there is *urbanism*, or the tendency for people to lead increasingly urban ways of life.

These three processes have tended to occur together through history, but they are separate processes. This is shown, for instance, in industrial countries such as Britain and the United States, where urbanisation has reached a peak and may even be declining, a situation which is called *counter-urbanisation*. However, even in these circumstances, individual cities may still be growing as a function of total population increase.

Similarly, with respect to the Third World, it is sometimes argued that the rapid influx of rural migrants, who are used to a rural way of life, is leading to a reduction in urbanism at a time when both urbanisation and urban growth are increasing rapidly. This is yet another indication of the special nature of current urban development in the Third World. In fact, it is more fitting to see cities in these regions as giving rise to new and different forms of urbanism.

2   MILLIONAIRE CITIES AND POOR PEOPLE

One of the clearest ways of appreciating the current scale of urban development in the Third World is to examine the growth of very large urban places within the region. Useful data concerning all world cities with more than 100 000 inhabitants are provided in the United Nations *Demographic Yearbook*.

Several geographers have used these data to chart the rise of *millionaire cities* from the early 1920s. Their results are summarised in Figure 1.2. In the 1920s, there were twenty-four cities in the world with more than one million inhabitants, housing 2.86 per cent of the world's population. By the early 1980s, the number of million cities had virtually increased tenfold, to 198, and they accounted for 11.36 per cent of world population.

Figure 1.2 demonstrates the increasing association of large cities with the tropical world. Each decade the average latitude of million cities has moved steadily toward the equator, from 44°30′ in the 1920s, to 34°07′ in the 1980s.

The growth of low latitude urbanisation is further demonstrated by the total number of million cities that are located between 0° and 35° north and south of the equator. In the 1960s,

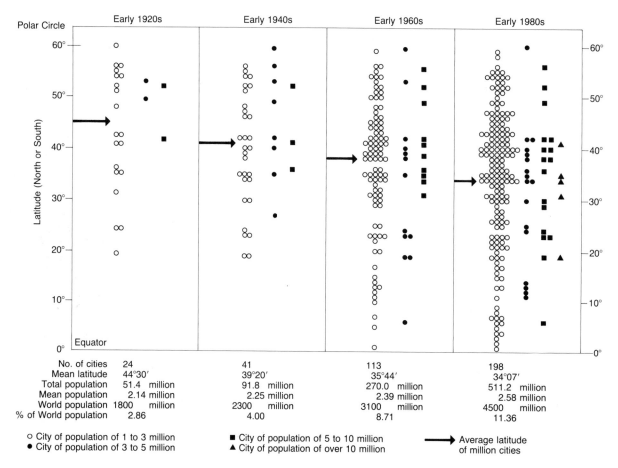

Figure 1.2 *The world distribution of million cities, early 1920s to early 1980s (based on A. Mountjoy, 1986)*

there were 52 out of the world total of 113, and these housed 45 per cent of all million city population. By the early 1980s, there were 98 such cities out of 198, and they accounted for 52 per cent of the total million city population.

Urbanisation, urban growth and associated million cities are occurring in the regions of the world where socio-economic conditions are generally at their poorest. The low latitudes are where the majority of the so called *Third World* countries are located.

The term *Third World* was originally used to signify countries which did not belong to the *First* *World* of capitalist or free-market nations, nor the *Second World* communist states. The Third World consisted of countries which had formerly come under the control of First World nations during the era of *colonialism*, which lasted from the fifteenth century through to the twentieth century when European countries brought many overseas territories under their direct control. Much has happened in the Third World in the period since 1945, and the term is now basically used to describe the *poorer countries* of the world which were formerly colonies of the major European nations.

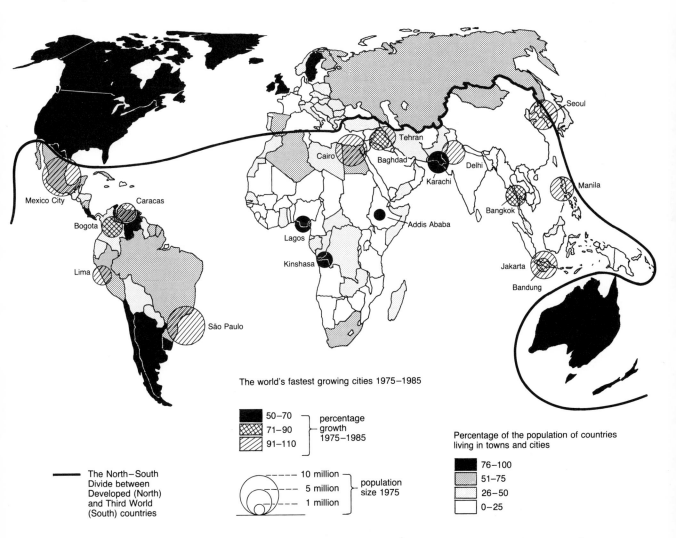

Figure 1.3 *World map showing the definition of the Third World, or South, and levels of urbanisation by country*

A commonly accepted geographical definition of the Third World is shown in Figure 1.3. The Third World is also referred to as the *South*, for the countries comprising it lie to the south of the line shown on the map. The Third World or South includes virtually all the states which make up Middle and Central America, the Caribbean, Africa, the Middle East and South and East Asia.

Figure 1.3 also shows the degree to which the various regions of the world are urbanised, and indicates the location of the world's fastest growing cities, all of them being located in the Third World. The United Nations projections for urbanisation by region between 1920 and 2000 are listed in Table 1.1.

By 1980, the world as a whole was nearly half urbanised. Levels of urbanisation ranged from 70 per cent for developed countries to 32 per cent for Third World nations. North America is the most highly urbanised continent, followed by Oceania, the Soviet Union and Europe in that order. In the Third World, Latin America is already showing a level of urbanisation which is approaching that of the First World. Although the remaining areas of the Third World stand out by virtue of their relatively low levels of urbanisation, they are currently urbanising at very rapid rates. By the year 2000, the overall level of urbanisation in the Third World will have reached 43 per cent.

But the true scale of the urban explosion in the Third World is only appreciated if the *absolute* numbers, in terms of urban growth, are examined rather than *relative* levels of urbanisation. It is

Table 1.1 Levels of urbanisation for major world regions, 1920–2000

	Population living in urban places (%)		
World region	*1920*	*1980*	*2000*
Less developed countries	10	32	43
East Asia	9	31	40
South Asia	9	25	35
Latin America	22	60	80
Africa	7	28	39
More developed countries	40	70	80
Europe	46	46	71
North America	52	65	87
Soviet Union	15	81	85
Oceania	47	68	80
WORLD	19	46	51

Source: United Nations, 1969.

Table 1.2 The largest cities in the world, 1950 and 2000

	1950			2000	
Rank	*City*	*Population (millions)*	*Rank*	*City*	*Population (millions)*
1	New York	12.3	1	Mexico City	31.0
2	London	10.4	2	São Paulo	25.8
3	Rhine-Ruhr	6.9	3	Shanghai	23.7
4	Tokyo	6.7	4	Tokyo	23.7
5	Shanghai	5.8	5	New York	22.4
6	Paris	5.5	6	Beijing	20.9
7	Buenos Aires	5.3	7	Rio de Janeiro	19.0
8	Chicago	4.9	8	Bombay	16.8
9	Moscow	4.8	9	Calcutta	16.4
10	Calcutta	4.6	10	Jakarta	15.7
11	Los Angeles	4.0	11	Los Angeles	13.9
12	Osaka	3.8	12	Seoul	13.7
13	Milan	3.6	13	Cairo	12.9
14	Bombay	3.0	14	Madras	12.7
15	Mexico City	3.0	15	Buenos Aires	12.1

Source: United Nations, 1985.

estimated that of a total world population of 6112 millions by the year 2000, some 3090 millions, or 51 per cent, will be living in urban places. In the developed world, 83 per cent of the population will be urbanised, amounting to 1010 million people. Whilst the overall level of urbanisation in the Third World will be 43 per cent, in absolute terms this represents a staggering 2080 million urban dwellers. By the year 2000, for every one person in a town or a city in the developed world, there will be two living in Third World cities.

These statistics are staggering. They indicate that the poor countries of the world have to find jobs, homes, schools, hospitals and social services for all these additional urban dwellers.

Table 1.2 lists the largest cities in the world in 1950 and those projected for the year 2000. By the turn of the century, New York and London will no longer be the largest cities in the world. Their places will have been taken by Mexico City, São Paulo and other Third World cities. Mexico City is projected to become the largest city on earth with a population over 30 million people. It is little wonder that at the moment, the role of cities in development is becoming an issue of major concern to politicians and planners.

3   HISTORICAL PERSPECTIVES: MERCANTILISM, COLONIALISM AND CAPITALISM

3.1 Urbanisation and social change

The manner in which the present-day pattern of rapid world urbanisation came about is complex. Understanding it requires a brief review of the development of human societies and the rise of the *world economy*. In his book, *City and Society: An Outline for Urban Geography*, Johnston recognises five broad changes in the structure of society (Figure 1.4).

From the emergence of human life some 3 million years ago, human groups were hunters and gatherers. During this era of the Old Stone Age the first human communities were small and people were equal. Goods and services were exchanged (*reciprocated*) and no ruling or elite group existed. These are referred to as *Reciprocal Societies*, and evidence shows that they simply cannot support cities.

Some 10 000 years BC the Agricultural or *Neolithic* Revolution occurred in various regions, when human groups started to farm the land on a permanent and settled basis. This allowed the land to support more people and eventually enabled people to specialise in the jobs they undertook. Religious and military power developed and gave rise to what are called *Rank Redistribution Societies*. These were communities in which positions of power and influence (*rank*)

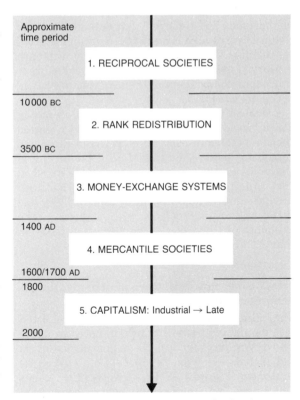

Figure 1.4 *Johnston's five stages in the development of human societies*

were limited to a few. As these changes occurred, an *Urban Revolution* gave rise to the development of the first cities. This happened in what are today Third World areas. These include Egypt, Iran, Iraq, India, China, Central America, and Nigeria.

Later, efforts to increase economic growth required trade between different communities and regions. This led to the establishment of a common exchange or money system. *Money Exchange Societies* led to a clearer social division of groups. There was a small ruling elite, and larger intermediate and lower groups.

The major development in global urbanisation and economic change was the evolution of the *Mercantile Society* within Europe. Trade allowed goods to be produced in the most appropriate areas. Merchants, people who buy and sell goods, became important agents in the rise of this system. This happened locally within Europe at first, but later started to occur across the oceans. European countries such as Portugal, Spain, Britain, France, Germany, Belgium, the Netherlands and Italy felt that economic growth required more land. Hence these nations started to colonise areas overseas from the fifteenth century onward. Coastal ports became very important components of the settlement system, acting as *gateways*.

Urbanisation started in many present-day Third World countries at this time and reflected the close economic association between European colonising powers, or the *Mother Country*, and their overseas colonies. Such towns were based on the collection and shipment of agricultural products and on administrative control. They had little or nothing to do with industry. The influence of this can still be witnessed today in many Third World countries.

3.2 The mercantile pattern of urbanisation: urban primacy

The influence of the Mercantile period is reflected in a distinctive pattern of urban places in many Third World countries. Their development is illustrated by Vance's model of *mercantile settlement* (Figure 1.5). This involves five stages which see an increasingly close connection between the colony and Mother Country.

In the first, the colonial power sends out search

parties to gain knowledge. If natural resources such as timber or fish are found, ships visit the area on a periodic basis and tap this natural harvest (Stage 2). At the third stage, settlers who produce staple agricultural products such as tobacco, sugar, coffee or rubber are established. These colonists depend on the import of manufactured goods from the home country, so a complex two-way economic flow occurs between the two areas. This serves to reduce the effective distance separating the colony and Mother Country. Stages 4 and 5 see the development of increasingly close relations between the two areas.

These mercantile forces gave rise to many coastal towns and cities, with other settlements growing on lines of trade into the interior. The existence of *urban primacy*, the growth of one or more very large cities, can also be explained in these historical terms. Primacy is typical of former colonies, especially those which are small, have low incomes, and have agricultural economies geared to export. Examination of the map of world population shows just how common this pattern is, and many countries in West Africa, South America and the Pacific show strong concentrations of coastal cities.

3.3 The Industrial Revolution and the rise of capitalism

The fifth and final societal stage in Figure 1.4 is *Capitalism*.

i) Urbanisation in the developed world

The industrial revolution occurred during the late eighteenth and early nineteenth centuries in Great Britain and the rest of Europe. The modern era of urbanisation started in 1800, and at that date only 3 per cent of the world's population was urban. Technical developments in the first stage of the industrial revolution up to 1830 contributed to increasing agricultural productivity and allowed rural population to decline.

At the same time, there was a rapid increase in demand for labour in the towns. Thus, a steady stream of migrants flowed from the countryside to the town. The main change was the use of non-animal based sources of energy and machinery. The steam engine, factory system and processes of mass production were all central to the industrial revolution.

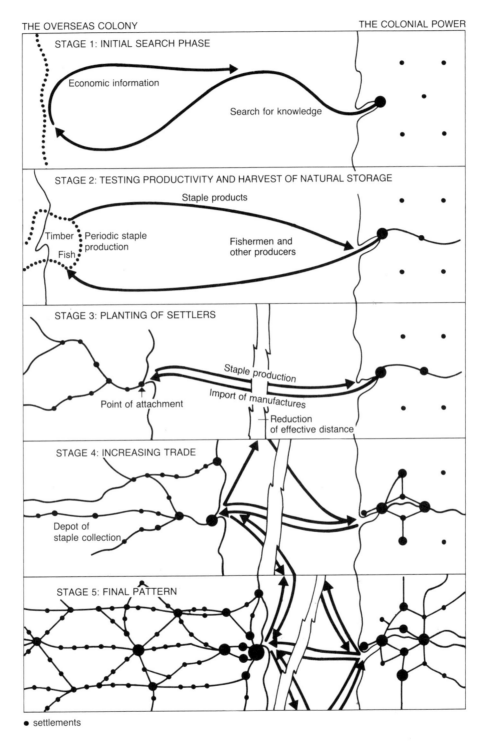

THE OVERSEAS COLONY

THE COLONIAL POWER

STAGE 1: INITIAL SEARCH PHASE

Economic information

Search for knowledge

STAGE 2: TESTING PRODUCTIVITY AND HARVEST OF NATURAL STORAGE

Staple products

Timber

Periodic staple production

Fish

Fishermen and other producers

STAGE 3: PLANTING OF SETTLERS

Staple production

Point of attachment

Import of manufactures

Reduction of effective distance

STAGE 4: INCREASING TRADE

Depot of staple collection

STAGE 5: FINAL PATTERN

● settlements

Figure 1.5 *The mercantile model of settlement patterns in a colony and the Mother Country (based on J. Vance, 1970)*

Industrialisation and urbanisation occurred together gradually over a century or more in Europe. Another important factor was that health conditions were relatively poor in the towns. Cities grew by people migrating to them (*in-migration*). In fact there was little or no *natural increase* in population, that is an excess of births over deaths.

The gradual increase in urbanisation described above is referred to as the *cycle of urbanisation*. This takes the form of a flattened s-shaped curve. The cycle is shown in Figure 1.6c. This can be looked at in association with the *demographic transition model* which looks at patterns of birth and death rates through time (Figure 1.6a).

The cycle of urbanisation and the demographic transition can be compared directly for developed countries. At the beginning of the nineteenth century, urbanisation was low and so was the rate of overall population growth. The era of most rapid urbanisation came in the early part of the nineteenth century, at a time when the death rate started to drop. As Britain moved into the

late expanding stage of the demographic transition, urbanisation had started to slow down appreciably, and on entry to the low fluctuating stage, intense urbanisation had run its course.

ii) Urbanisation in the Third World

The majority of Third World countries are not following the same pattern of urbanisation and demographic change (Figures 1.6d and b). Instead their rates of urbanisation are taking place at a faster pace and with Third World populations growing at around 2 per cent per annum, urbanisation is working on a much larger base population. In the 1940s and 1950s the average gain in population of Third World cities was 4.5 per cent per annum. In comparison, for most European countries during their periods of fastest urbanisation, the average gain per year had been less than half this, at 2.1 per cent. By the 1950s, Third World cities were growing at an average of 5.1 per cent per annum. Many individual urban areas were growing much more quickly than this, as shown by Table 1.3. Abidjan in West Africa, for

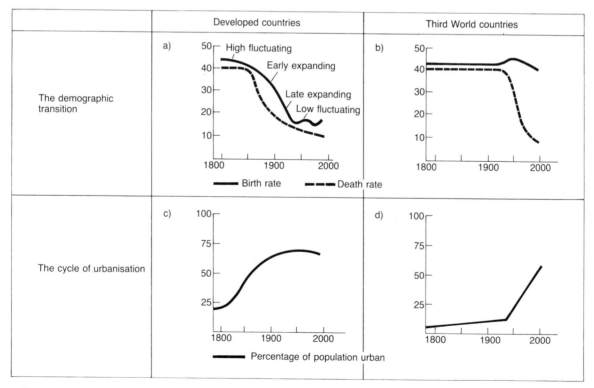

Figure 1.6 *The cycle of urbanisation and demographic transition for developed and developing countries*

example, recorded a growth rate of 11 per cent per year. At this rate a city will double its population in only seven years.

Table 1.3 Selected examples of the rapid growth of Third World cities during the period 1960–70

City and country	Annual increase of population (%)
Dar es Salaam, Tanzania	9.0
Kampala, Uganda	9.2
Kinshasa, Zaire	10.0
Abidjan, Ivory Coast	11.0
Seoul, South Korea	8.0
Bangkok, Thailand	6.0
Karachi, Pakistan	5.6
Katmandu, Nepal	7.9
Cairo, Egypt	4.1
Guatemala City, Guatemala	5.0
Mexico City, Mexico	5.0
Caracas, Venezuela	5.5
São Paulo, Brazil	6.4
Bogota, Colombia	7.0
Lima, Peru	5.1

Source: World Bank, 1972.

The most important factor in this has been better medical facilities in the post-war period, whilst birth rates have remained at traditionally high levels. It is the combination of traditionally high birth rates and low death rates that is leading to such rapid urban growth. Thus, many Third World cities are growing by *natural increase* and *in-migration* in almost equal proportions, something that was largely unheard of during the industrial period (Table 1.4).

Table 1.4 Rural-to-urban migrants as a percentage of population increase for a selection of Third World cities between 1951 and 1969

City	Period	Migrants as a percentage of total population increase
Caracas	1960–66	50
São Paulo	1950–60	72
Bogota	1956–66	33
Bombay	1951–61	52
Lagos	1952–62	75
Nairobi	1961–69	50
Seoul	1955–65	63
Djakarta	1961–68	59

Source: World Bank, 1972.

But rural-to-urban migration is also occurring very quickly and it is estimated that as many as 50 000 people migrate to cities in the Third World every day. Such migration may be seen as the outcome of push and pull factors at the present location and the future possible one as shown in Figure 1.7a. If the balance between the pluses (*attracting forces*) and the minuses (*repelling forces*) lies in favour of the large city, migration will occur. Evidence shows that people from the countryside often migrate to the largest city in stages. This is called *chain* or *step-migration* (Figure 1.7b).

It must be stressed that the pluses or advantages of urban living for the individual are often *perceived* rather than real. For example, it is true that on average, wage levels are higher in the city than the countryside. However, very large proportions of the inhabitants are unemployed on an almost permanent basis.

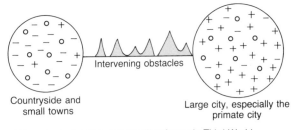

Countryside and small towns

Large city, especially the primate city

a) Perceived attracting and repelling forces in Third World urban migration

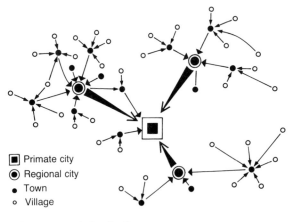

■ Primate city
◉ Regional city
● Town
○ Village

b) Step-wise or chain migration

Figure 1.7 *Aspects of rural-to-urban migration in Third World countries*

4   DEPENDENCY THEORY AND THIRD WORLD URBANISATION

In the 1950s and 1960s, it was a popular view that Third World countries were poor because they had simply failed to keep up with the progress made by developed countries. It was believed that if the right steps could be followed, economic development could be spread to backward areas. This approach is referred to as *modernisation theory*.

Whilst some argue that the process of European colonisation of the traditional world by the Spanish, Portuguese, British, Germans, Belgians, French, Dutch and Italians represented the initial spread of global *economic development*, others are more critical and maintain that looked at historically, it represents a form of *exploitation*.

Overseas countries were developed as the producers of staple crops such as sugar, bananas, rubber and tea, often using the *plantation system*. Large profits were made, but most of the money and resources were sent back to the Mother Country. This is a major issue concerning the past which shapes political views of current urbanisation processes and patterns.

What cannot be ignored is that the evolution of the developed and less developed areas of the world has been very closely interrelated over the past five hundred years. In this regard, urban primacy and urban poverty in the Third World cannot be interpreted as the outcome of countries somehow failing to keep up with development. Rather these conditions reflect the way that these countries have been brought into the world economic system dominated by capitalism. *Capitalism* is the economic system which is based on the private ownership of resources and factors of production.

This latter argument has given rise to a set of ideas concerning economic development and urbanisation. This is called *dependency theory* and was developed by an American economist, Frank, in the 1970s. Basically, Frank argued that backwardness has not occurred as a result of the separation of developing countries from advanced capitalist countries. Frank argued that the more that underdeveloped countries have been associated with advanced capitalist countries, the more underdeveloped they have become. According to Frank, Third World countries have joined the world economic system at the bottom and have been held in a dependent position. Dependency theory is a *Marxist* alternative to the views of modernisation theory. Marxist ideas are those which come from the writings of Karl Marx (1818–1883). Marx took a strongly historical view of the process of world economic change.

Dependency theory has done a service in stimulating much debate about the reasons for Third World poverty. The theory also has a very strong geographical basis. This is because Frank saw the world economy as being controlled by large cities in capitalist countries, like London, Paris and New York. These he called *Metropoles*, and from them he saw a chain of dependency stretching right down to backward rural areas in Third World countries.

Colonial territories were organised to produce primary products such as tea, coffee, sugar, rubber and tobacco for European markets. The prices for these goods were kept relatively low by these markets. Farm labourers were paid relatively little for their work. Thus excess profits were extracted from them and moved to the primate city or *satellite*. From here the profits were eventually transferred to the European metropoles. A simplified representation of dependency is shown in Figure 1.8. The approach provides one set of ideas about why some countries are poor and why the rural areas within them are even poorer. Dependency theory is sometimes referred to as a model of the *development of underdevelopment*.

Because of their political views, some people may find it very difficult to accept all of Frank's ideas. But as noted previously, by definition, the description *Third World* means both former colonies and poor countries, for in so many cases these two conditions do go together. There are of course exceptions, and countries such as Australia, Canada, the United States and New Zealand are all former colonies which have become highly developed.

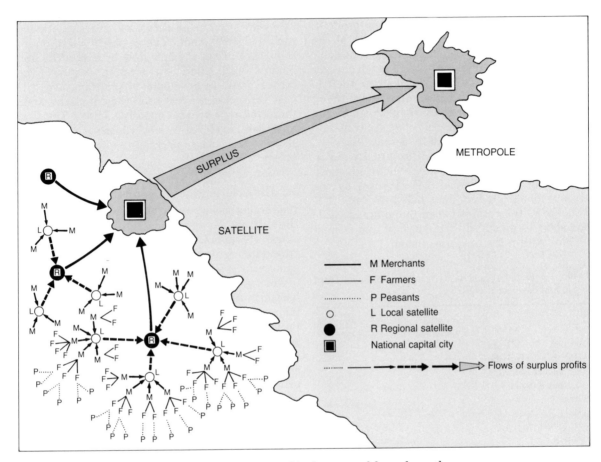

Figure 1.8 *Some geographical aspects of dependency theory*

Others stress that however true historically, dependency theories must not overlook the strong influence of *internal* or *national* factors within countries. These include repressive, authoritarian and military governments, political instability and coups as well as politicians or particular social groups acting in a corrupt fashion. They argue that recent political, social and economic conditions have served to hold countries back as much as anything else.

Both *internationalist (dependency)* and *nationalist* interpretations of underdevelopment

are of importance. Further, the relative contribution of these two influences to poverty will vary from one country to another. As with most global issues, looking for one single cause is likely to be far too simplistic. But if the importance of history in relation to urbanisation and global development is appreciated, this opens up a new and more challenging way of looking at these vital issues. As will be seen later, such an approach suggests very different policies to those suggested by modernisation theory.

5   CITIES AND INEQUALITIES

5.1 The basic issues

Since 1945, the arguments considered in Section 4 about urban areas and economic progress have influenced both thinking and policy at the regional scale in Third World countries. The basic issue is relatively simple. Although much poverty is to be found within Third World cities, they do show higher average incomes, standards of living and production levels than their surrounding rural areas. Such differences between towns and the countryside are referred to as *inequalities*.

Significantly, these inequalities are greater in many Third World countries than in advanced ones. Some impression of this is given by the gross regional product data listed in Table 1.5. This shows the ratio between the value of goods and services produced by the richest and poorest regions within the countries listed.

Table 1.5 Regional inequalities in a sample of Third World and developed countries

Country	Ratio of Gross Regional Product between the richest and poorest regions
Developed countries:	
United Kingdom	1.43
France	2.09
Italy	2.20
Netherlands	1.56
Japan	2.92
Developing countries:	
Brazil	10.14
Thailand	6.34
Iran	10.07
India	2.24
Venezuela	5.72

Source: B. Renard, 1981.

In Brazil, the richest region of the country has a gross regional product over ten times that of the poorest. Indeed, in the majority of Third World countries, this index is well over 5. By contrast, in developed countries such as the United Kingdom, the Netherlands and Japan, the difference between the richest and poorest regions often tends to be in the order of 1.5 to 3.

But the fact that cities are on average richer can be interpreted in two very different ways. One view argues that towns and cities create and spread development. The opposite view maintains that urban regions grow by exploiting and holding back their surrounding regions. The central issue in development planning over the past three decades has been the debate between those taking up these opposing views. The first approach is related to *modernisation theory*; the second has close parallels with *dependency theory*.

5.2 Cities as engines of growth

This crucial debate was raised as early as 1955 by Hoselitz in a paper, *Generatives and parasitic cities*. He noted that urban places can either stimulate growth in their wider regions (*generative cities*), or can reduce such growth (*parasitic cities*). Hoselitz subscribed to the basically optimistic view that although the majority of colonial cities were parasitic at first, later they spread economic benefits in a generative manner.

The predominant view of the 1950s was that cities indeed played such a generative role in bringing development to poor and backward regions. This view was strongly taken by the American economist Hirschman in his book, *The Strategy of Economic Development* (1958). In this he maintained that widening inequalities are an inevitable part of the early stages of economic development, as one region grows fast. However, increasing concentration, or *polarisation* as Hirschman called it, would eventually lead to the spreading of growth to poorer areas. This process was called *trickling-down*.

The important point is that Hirschman maintained that this would happen without politicians doing anything, so that all governments need to do is to encourage the growth of major industries and development would inevitably spread. Thereby, development was equated with urban-industrial growth, exactly as had been the case in the First World during the Industrial Revolution.

Many Third World governments came to regard the establishment of industries, making goods which were formerly imported, and the attraction of overseas manufacturing plants as central to development. These are referred to as *import-substitution*, and *enclave manufacturing* respectively. During this era it was strongly believed that backward regions could be developed by establishing new urban places at strategic locations within them. These new urban-industrial complexes are referred to as *new towns*, *growth poles* and *growth centres*, depending on their precise size and location. A host of Third World nations, including Malaysia, Mexico, Chile and Kenya have followed this approach.

5.3 Cities and uneven development

But even when these ideas were being put forward and applied in practice, there were writers who were less sure of the close relation between urban-industrial development and economic progress.

A very important writer in this connection is the Swedish development economist, Myrdal. In his book *Economic Theory and Underdeveloped Areas* he argued that capitalist development is generally characterised by marked inequalities. He stressed that economic growth follows a principle of *cumulative causation*, whereby once economic success is established in an area or city it promotes further local development. Surrounding areas or areas away from this growth lose out. Myrdal called this the *backwash effect*. Although it was accepted that urban-industrial areas do generate *spread* effects, such as increased demand for resources and agricultural products, it was maintained that these never match the force of the backwash effect. Myrdal took the generally pessimistic view that only government policy can prevent the establishment and maintenance of extreme inequality between regions, quite the reverse of Hirschman.

5.4 The core-periphery model

The crucial debate between the Myrdal and Hirschman schools of thought is reflected in what is perhaps the best-known model of regional development. This is the *core-periphery* framework provided by the American planner, Friedmann.

The model recognises four stages in the development of countries (Figure 1.10). The first

Figure 1.9 *Caracas, Venezuela. Cities have always been seen as centres of change and development, but the degree to which this is spread to the wider region has been debated*

two stages are associated with the sort of increasing concentration that Myrdal developed. Stage 1 represents the pre-industrial era and is associated with a number of isolated, self-sufficient, local communities. As a second stage, due to external factors such as the establishment of a colony, growth advances rapidly in one major primate city. This urban core (C) feeds on the rest of the nation so that the periphery (P) is drained of skilled workers and other resources.

At Stage 3, the model includes Hirschman-type spread effects, and sub-cores (SC) develop and the poorly developed peripheries between urban areas get smaller and smaller (P_1-P_4). With time, the theoretical outcome is a pattern of relatively even development and a smooth progression of urban places. This is called a *rank-size* distribution of cities.

Friedmann developed his model after studying the pattern of economic growth in Venezuela. Here strong growth focused on the primate capital of Caracas after the development of the oil industry in the 1920s.

But even at the time of presenting his model in 1966, Friedmann noted that there was one major point relating to history which needed to be made. He noted that the change from Stage 2 (single strong centre) to Stage 3 (peripheral sub-centres) rarely happens without government involvement. Certainly enough evidence exists to support the view most development writers put forward today, that *inequalities are not a temporary event on the road to an even pattern of modernisation and development.*

STAGE 1   Independent local centres/no hierarchy

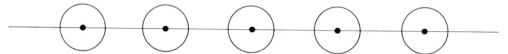

STAGE 2   A single strong centre

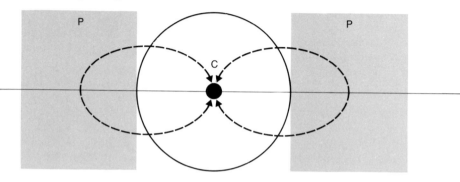

STAGE 3   A single national centre with strong peripheral sub-centres

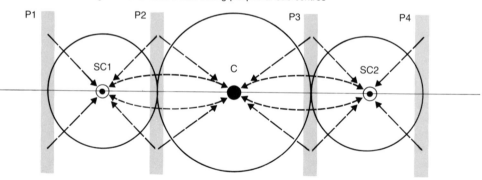

STAGE 4   A functionally interdependent system of cities

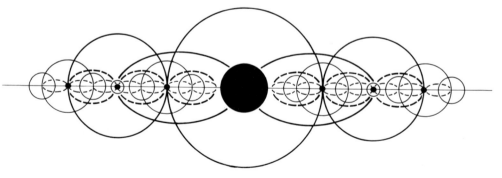

Figure 1.10 *The core-periphery model of development (based on J. Friedmann, 1966)*

6 MODERN PATTERNS OF CONSUMPTION AND PRODUCTION IN THIRD WORLD CITIES

Figure 1.11 Part of the modern city centre of Caracas, Venezuela

In looking at patterns of urbanisation today, it is important to understand that cities both concentrate and spread new developments at the same time.

In a book called *Theatres of Accumulation*, two geographers, Armstrong and McGee, have recently emphasised that modern Third World cities spread and concentrate different things. Under an entirely free-market or capitalist system, dependent countries import goods, fashions and ways of doing things from developed countries. Indeed, years of assuming that to develop means to be like the countries of Europe and North America has left many Third World governments and people inclined to think that things produced overseas are better than those produced at home.

Multinational corporations (MNCs), large worldwide firms which have branch plants in many countries, are frequently key agents in this, selling soft drinks, fast foods, cigarettes, alcoholic drinks, popular music and styles of dress. Cities, especially primate capital cities, are the points at which these imported products and ways of life are introduced and spread in Third World countries.

Thus, it can be argued that in dependent countries, cities have often served to spread patterns of consumption that are based on Western lifestyles and values. It is largely for this reason that the wealthy parts of many Third World cities look very much like New York, Miami, London, Paris or indeed any other world city (see Figure 1.11). Patterns of consumption in Third World countries are tending to *converge* on a global norm or average.

On the other hand, production, the creation of goods, is tending to *diverge* at the global scale. Due to world competition, some countries are almost exclusively producing agricultural crops, while others are mainly producing different types of manufactures. In this way, it is argued that Third World cities are tending to concentrate production and large multinational companies are playing a prominent role in this. In other words, where industrial plants are located, often foreign-owned ones, they tend to be concentrated in urban areas and there are few spread effects to the surrounding areas. Often these industries use much capital and machinery and provide relatively few jobs, as, for instance, in the manufacture of sports equipment and electrical goods. This view of cities is related to dependency theory. It sees cities as areas which are holding the rest of the country back, and not as centres of development that will be spread quickly.

7   TOP-DOWN AND BOTTOM-UP STRATEGIES OF DEVELOPMENT

7.1 Top-down planning

Where development has been planned in Third World countries in the period since 1945, the accent has so often been placed on the establish-

ment of industry in urban regions. In recent years this has come to be described as *top-down planning*. Such approaches are top-down in the sense that they believe economic growth will

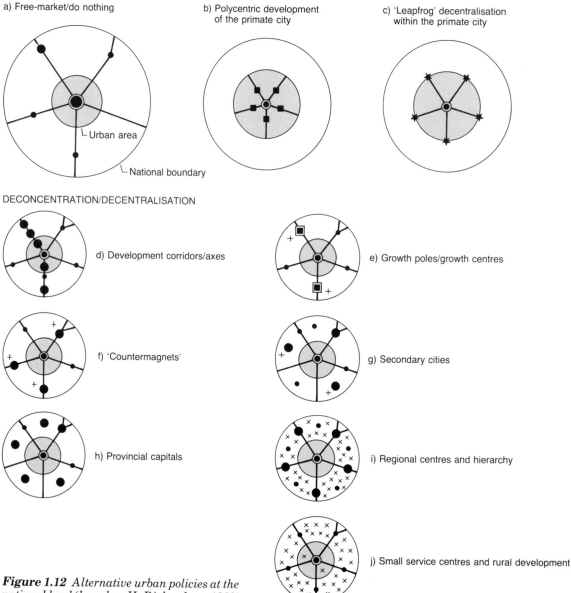

CONCENTRATED URBANISATION

a) Free-market/do nothing

b) Polycentric development of the primate city

c) 'Leapfrog' decentralisation within the primate city

Urban area

National boundary

DECONCENTRATION/DECENTRALISATION

d) Development corridors/axes

e) Growth poles/growth centres

f) 'Countermagnets'

g) Secondary cities

h) Provincial capitals

i) Regional centres and hierarchy

j) Small service centres and rural development

Figure 1.12 *Alternative urban policies at the national level (based on H. Richardson, 1982)*

spread naturally from the largest urban places right down to the smallest villages.

Even when the need to move people, jobs and activities to other regions is agreed by all, this process of *decentralisation* or *deconcentration* can be carried out in very different ways. In simple terms there are different degrees of decentralisation. Some idea of this is given by Figure 1.12. Apart from the *do nothing* strategy (1.12a) there are two examples of local decentralisation within the region of the primate city (1.12b and c). Figures 1.12d to 1.12j show various forms of deconcentration-decentralisation at the regional scale. These vary from the relative concentration of development axes to small dispersed service centres and rural development. The latter approach, for example, has been implemented in Tanzania.

In practice, planning policies in most Third World countries have generally involved creating new towns and urban growth poles in less developed regions. The critics of such policies note that these responses are often not a solution to the problem. They argue that they merely replace over-concentration in one area with new pockets of over-concentration in other regions, the very thing that caused the problem in the first place.

7.2 Bottom-up planning

Since the mid-1970s, a growing number of development experts have stressed that a new form of development planning is needed in the Third World. In many respects the approach requires the adoption of a new definition of *development* itself. Specifically, development is not to be regarded as *economic progress* alone, that is, increasing incomes and the production of more goods. Rather, development should be seen as involving *social change*, for example, improving the quality of life or increasing democracy and self-expression.

The new approach to development and planning is called *bottom-up planning*. This maintains that development and change must come from the lower levels of the economy, and rural people must be involved in the process of deciding how such change is to occur. The approach stresses the everyday needs of the people and focuses on the extreme importance of agriculture and programmes of rural development.

One objective of this approach is, of course, to reduce dependency. Rather than the emphasis of development being placed on urban-industrialisation, the emphasis is on the creation of rural employment. Instead of prizing imported goods and ways of life, local and traditional ways of doing things are respected and encouraged. Rather than economic factors, social considerations are brought to the fore. Instead of the consumption of goods being all important, the accent is placed firmly on the production of the things that are required by all, such as food, clothing and shelter.

8   NEW PERSPECTIVES ON DEVELOPMENT AND URBANISATION

8.1 Fulfilment of basic needs

The production of the daily requirements of life within the country before more sophisticated goods are imported from abroad is referred to as fulfilling *basic needs*. This can only be achieved if the national economy and the regions comprising it are at least partly closed to trade with more advanced countries and regions. Those putting forward such a view of development stress that it is only by increasing self-sufficiency and reliance that Third World countries can hope to break the chains of dependency and the outward flows of surplus profits that have characterised their development since the era of colonialism.

Although the *bottom-up* approach stresses agriculture and rural areas to begin with, it is envisaged that later, the economy can be diversified and non-agricultural activities introduced. But it is maintained that at this stage, it is not essential for industry to be located in urban areas, as assumed in the past. Equally, it is recognised that cities can be based on agriculture and agro-industries, just as many were in earlier time periods. Thus, the approach is also referred to as involving the principles of *agropolitan development.*

8.2 Sustainable development

Very recently, another closely related concept of development has emerged – that of *sustainable development.* Sustainable development emphasises that recent efforts to develop Third World countries have been associated with severe problems, many of which have involved the destruction of the environment. Examples of this include the clearance of tropical rainforests, increases in soil erosion, and widespread pollution due to inappropriate programmes of agricultural and industrial development.

At a popular level, movements such as *Band Aid* and *Live Aid* have increased awareness of famine, hunger and malnutrition in Third World countries. Many developing nations now face a debt crisis, because they have taken out loans from developed countries at high interest rates in order to implement development projects in the past. Countries such as Mexico and Brazil are now facing huge debt crises. This may mean that some have little option but to consider any means of earning money, even if this involves harming the environment.

The approach argues that, as a result, many past efforts to develop have not been sustainable; they have taken what is on offer from the environment, knowing that in the not too distant future this will no longer be possible as resources are used up. Agricultural schemes are needed which have stood the test of time and which are based on local custom. Industry needs to be less harmful to the environment and towns and cities must grow in a way that helps the poor. Stated simply, a far better match between development and the environment is required.

In all of this it is clear that a new view of the role of towns and cities in Third World development is emerging. Urban areas are no longer viewed without question as the points from which modernisation, created by Western-style industry, will be efficiently and evenly spread. In some circumstances, a larger number of smaller towns and cities might be appropriate. Certainly, much greater attention has to be paid to developing the rural areas of Third World countries if more appropriate patterns of economic and social development are to be promoted. These approaches are not anti-urban as such, rather they suggest a flexible way of regarding towns and cities as parts of an integrated view of development.

9   MODELS OF THIRD WORLD CITY STRUCTURE

Just as thinking about the role of urbanisation and of towns and cities at the regional scale in Third World countries has undergone change, so have views concerning patterns of day-to-day life within them. Are fast-growing cities in developing countries becoming more and more like cities in Europe or North America, or do they show their own distinctive patterns? What can be done to improve the all-too-apparent shortages of both adequate housing and jobs?

With respect to the first question, Third World cities are seen by some as being essentially the same as *pre-industrial cities.* The concept of the pre-industrial city was fully explored by Sjoberg

in the 1960s. According to Sjoberg, the most important characteristic of such cities is that before the onset of industrialisation, towns and cities tend to show a complete reversal of the social patterns that are found in today's modern cities. Instead of the wealthy or elite groups living toward the edge of the city and the poor residing at the centre as tends to happen in industrial cities, the rich live close to the urban core. This is mainly because pre-industrial cities are based on walking, so that access to the city centre is highly prized.

The pre-industrial pattern is broadly summarised in Figure 1.13a. In the diagram below it,

a) THE PREINDUSTRIAL CITY (after Sjoberg)

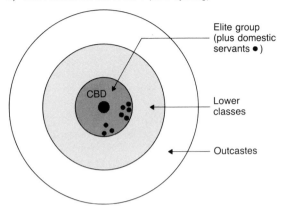

Elite group
(plus domestic
servants ●)

Lower
classes

Outcastes

b) THE INDUSTRIAL CITY

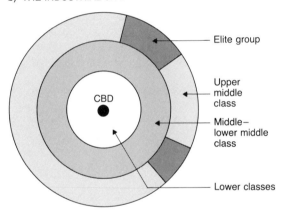

Elite group

Upper
middle
class

Middle–
lower middle
class

Lower classes

c) LATIN AMERICAN CITY STRUCTURE (after Griffin and Ford)

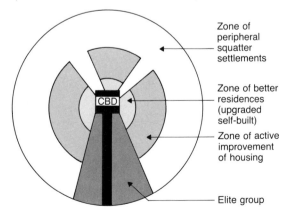

Zone of
peripheral
squatter
settlements

Zone of better
residences
(upgraded
self-built)

Zone of active
improvement
of housing

Elite group

Figure 1.13 *The structure of Third World cities*

a model of the Western or industrial city is shown (Figure 1.13b). There is evidence to suggest that the pre-industrial model fits quite well in the case of a number of Third World cities, particularly colonial cities of Africa and Asia.

Recent evidence suggests that this pattern is fast becoming less typical, especially in large Latin American cities such as Lima in Peru, Bogota in Colombia and Caracas in Venezuela. In these cities, the elite groups have tended to desert the centre of the city and now occupy one or more sectors of the outer urban area (Figure 1.14).

This trend has been mapped into a general model of Latin American cities by two geographers. The Griffin and Ford model proposed in 1980 is shown in Figure 1.13c. The most important aspect is the development of a high quality *commercial spine* which extends out from the *Central Business District (CBD)*. Along this spine the best shops, theatres, office buildings, restaurants, musuems, parks and zoos are located. Clustered around it in the form of a wedge are the residences of the elite. Because of the car and other forms of rapid transit, many Third World cities are becoming like Western cities.

In the other areas of the city, residential patterns remain basically pre-industrial. The inner city is still looked upon favourably by many middle-income families and the zone of maturity consists of homes which have slowly been improved. With distance out, houses tend to become more recent and poorer in quality, until the major new squatter settlements are found on the edge of the city.

An example of this type of structure is shown in the case of Bogota, Colombia. The land use map, reproduced in Figure 1.14, shows the commercial spine extending out from the CBD, and around it are the homes of the wealthy. All of this gives rise to a strong contrast between the rich and the poor in Third World cities.

It cannot be argued that the Latin American model fits cities in all other areas of the Third World, but it does show that things are changing. The rise of the motor car has much to do with these trends. In this manner, changes in city structure can be interpreted as yet a further instance of the process of increasingly similar patterns of consumption around the world, in this instance of land, roads and cars. But in other ways, elements of the pre-industrial era remain. In this case too, it appears sensible to conclude that Third World cities are developing in their own clear manner. This will vary from region to region, and the Griffin and Ford model gives some impression as to what this has entailed in one continent.

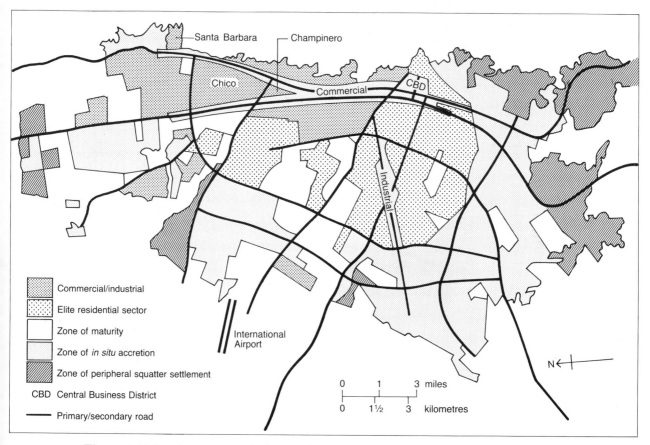

Figure 1.14 *Land use patterns in Bogota, Colombia (based on E. Griffin and L. Ford, 1980)*

10 HOUSING IN THIRD WORLD CITIES: FROM RAGS TO RICHES?

10.1 Slums of despair?

The majority of people living in Third World cities are unable to purchase houses which have been professionally surveyed and built. Indeed, it must not be forgotten that there are many thousands of people who are so poor that they sleep in the streets, as in Indian cities such as Calcutta, Bombay and Delhi. Others live in slums and tenement areas. It is generally accepted that perhaps as many as half the city dwellers of the Third World live in housing which may be regarded as sub-standard.

Housing areas which have been built by the poor themselves are generally referred to as *shanty towns*. In many instances, people build on land that they do not own, or on which they do not have the permission of planners to build. The areas which result are called *squatter settlements*. Both shanty towns and squatter settlements are the outcome of *self-help* (Figure 1.15).

Although conditions vary greatly from one self-built area to another, often houses do not have water taps and proper toilets. Residents may collect water from a communal standpipe, or they may even have to purchase supplies brought in by truck from outside. The individual dwellings are frequently packed close together and there are often no roads and only muddy paths between them. These types of settlement account for nearly a third to a half of the total population in many cities (Table 1.6).

Table 1.6 The extent of shanty towns, squatter settlements and slums in a selection of Third World cities

City and country	Shanty dwellers, squatters and slum dwellers as a proportion of the total city population (%)
Dar es Salaam, Tanzania	36
Calcutta, India	33
Jakarta, Indonesia	25
Karachi, Pakistan	33
Rio de Janeiro, Brazil	27
Santiago, Chile	25
Buenaventura, Colombia	80
Mexico City, Mexico	46
Lima, Peru	36
Caracas, Venezuela	35
Maracaibo, Venezuela	50

Source: World Bank, 1972.

The common view held in the 1940s and 1950s was that these settlements were a problem and that they should be demolished. This happened in many Third World cities and the residents were forced out of the homes they had built. They either became homeless or they were put into government housing schemes where they could not pay the rents. In Manila in the Philippines nearly 3000 shacks were demolished by the government in a two-week period. During the time when development experts were following closely the ideas of modernisation theory, it is not

Figure 1.15 *Self-help houses in front of a new tower block, Delhi, India*

surprising that many planners and politicians regarded shanty towns and squatter settlements as an admission of failure.

It was often argued that shanty towns and squatter settlements were full of people who had just migrated to the city from the countryside in search of a job. Clearing them would help dissuade other rural migrants.

But the work of geographers and others has shown clearly that in many instances this is not the case. One such study, of Montego Bay, the second-largest town in Jamaica, is considered as a good example. This was carried out in 1972 when the town had a population of 50 000 and there were ten shanty towns. These were mainly located some 4–6 km distant from the urban centre.

It was found that the majority of the people had lived in the shanty towns for a considerable time, the average being 11 years. More than 75 per cent had been born in Montego Bay itself. They were not rootless rural migrants who were flocking to the shanty areas. The work indicated that new arrivals to the city from the countryside at first generally live in the inner city in rented slum tenements. They do so in order to find work. It is only when they have found a job and become established that they move to a shanty town.

These migration patterns are shown in Figure 1.16 which is a simplified map of Montego Bay. The people concerned do this in order to avoid paying high rents. They also want the opportunity to build their own homes as and when their savings allow and to improve the lives of their children.

This type of finding has been mapped into a general model of the nature of squatter settlements. This is reproduced in Figure 1.17, and shows that although in the case of some cities, people do move directly from the countryside and small towns to squatter areas, more frequently, they migrate to the city centre first. This is frequently the case in Latin America, Caribbean and many Asian cities.

The model also gives a simplified idea of the location of squatter settlements. The city centre

with all its job opportunities is obviously the principal attracting force. As the urban area expands, such settlements may be pushed outward to the edge of the city. Other important site factors for squatter settlements are good water supplies and tolerable relief. However, as the city grows, some people may accept poor sites without water to be near to the city centre.

10.2 Slums of hope?

As a result of knowledge such as this, since the 1960s, a new and much more positive view has been taken of squatter settlements and shanty towns. It is a rags to riches story in several senses. Rather than being described as *urban cancers, festering sores* and *slums of despair*, these areas are now often seen as *slums of hope*.

This view emphasises the urban poor as

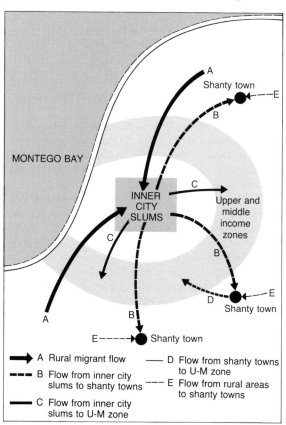

Figure 1.16 Patterns of migration in Montego Bay, Jamaica (based on A. Eyre, 1972)

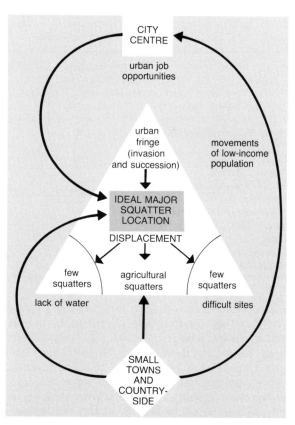

Figure 1.17 A model of the location of squatter settlements and shanty towns and movements to them (based on D. Dwyer, 1975)

building their own homes to make the best of an often desparate situation. They do so in order to avoid paying crippling rents and because governments are unable or unwilling to house them. In so doing, they take this immense burden from the shoulders of the state.

This perspective also stresses that housing problems stem from poverty and inequality in society as a whole. Squatting in particular does not just result from rapid migration to the city and over-urbanisation. The ownership of land by a few rich people, or indeed by the church, the army or the state itself, can be a crucial factor in promoting squatting.

Politicians are often closely involved with squatter settlements. They may suggest that groups build houses on government-owned land. In doing this they hope to gain the votes of the squatters at the next election and at the same time cause a potential embarrassment to the government. When squatter settlements have been established, politicians may turn a blind eye to their illegality in return for support. They may also help in the provision of essential services such as water, electricity, schools and the like on the same basis.

An English planner and architect, John Turner, worked for over eight years in Peru, in cities such as Lima. It has been his ideas that have done more than anything to change the views of people, governments and even inter-national agencies such as the World Bank and the United States Agency for Development (USAID). He argued that the *barriadas* or squatter settlements should not be seen as slums but as building sites.

The most important message that Turner put across was that such settlements improve progressively over time. Houses that were at first constructed from straw matting later acquired walls, paved streets and services. The people developed them into thriving communities. Such areas were not inhabited by dishonest and lazy people, but by people doing their very best to help themselves.

The clearest indication of Turner's basic ideas are contained in a simple model of the housing needs of poor people in Third World cities. This is shown in Figure 1.18. This stresses that there are very different housing groups in such cities.

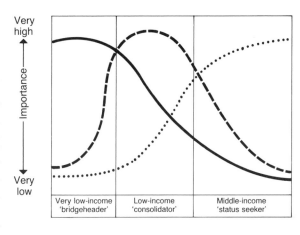

Figure 1.18 *Turner's model of the housing needs of different groups in Third World cities*

First there are the very-low income groups, or what Turner called *Bridgeheaders*. They are the people who have perhaps only just arrived in the city. They need to be close to the city centre in order to find a job. They are less bothered about permanent ownership or high standards of amenity. Secondly, there are low-income *Consolidators* who have lived in the area for some time and already have a job. For this group, permanent ownership and the chance to extend and improve a house is vital (Figure 1.18). Location and modern amenities are of less importance to members of this group and they tend to become squatters. Thus the model helps stress once more that people who have just migrated to the city are less likely to be found living in shanty towns than those who have lived there for some considerable time. Finally, it is only when individuals reach middle-income levels that modern standards of amenity become more important than location and ownership.

There is much evidence to show that if the conditions are right, shanty towns are improved or *consolidated* over time in the way Turner says. This has certainly happened in Latin American cities such as Lima in Peru. People have to be given the permanent ownership of the land on which they are living, and of course they need to have incomes which allow them to spend on their houses over time, even if only at a slow rate.

These ideas have also been very influential in the field of public policy and planning. Once such views are accepted, it becomes clear that the government must help the people to build for themselves. This may be achieved by providing the legal title to land, small loans at low rates of interest, building materials, technical assistance with building or essential communal services. The overall policy is referred to as *Aided Self-Help* (*ASH*). Examples of the approaches involved (squatter upgrading, site and service schemes and core housing) will be provided in Part II of this book (page 31).

11   THE INFORMAL SECTOR AND EMPLOYMENT

Without jobs, people in Third World cities will not be able to maintain and improve their homes, nor will they be in a position to support their families in an adequate manner. The fact that urban development is generally running ahead of industrialisation means that there are relatively few jobs in Third World cities.

Not only are there people without jobs, that is *unemployed*, there are also those who are *under-employed* and those who are *misemployed*. In the first of these, many people are found doing a job that could be done by far fewer. In the second, people may be found to be misemployed in the sense of being employed in ways that add little to social welfare. Examples of the latter include scavenging, prostitution, and involvement in drugs. It is obviously impossible to count the number of people who are underemployed and misemployed, but often unemployment rates run as high as 15–20 per cent of the urban labour force.

Just as people are building their own houses, many are also providing their own jobs. Typical examples are those who set up small *cottage industries* in squatter settlements, providing, for instance, tyre repair services and making furniture. Other examples include shoe shining, car cleaners, street traders and taxi drivers. These are the productive equivalents of shanty housing and they are the only hope that many people have of making a living in Third World cities.

Since the early 1970s, such activities have been referred to as making up an *informal sector* of the economy. The main features of this are defined in Figure 1.20. Typically, these enterprises are

Figure 1.19 *The informal sector: a furniture maker in Castries, St Lucia*

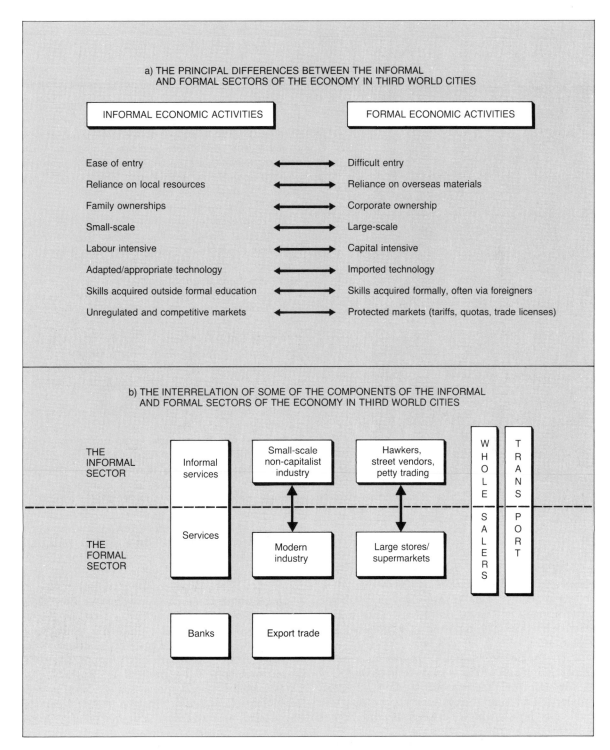

Figure 1.20 *Characteristics of the informal and formal sectors of the economy of Third World cities*

Figure 1.21 *The informal sector: painting learner driver signs in St John's, Antigua*

problem rather than an innovative response to the wider social, economic and political problems of poverty and inequality. People spoke of the *traditional* and *modern* sectors of the economy and argued that part of the development problem was to make the former like the latter. This thesis of *dualism* is similar to modernisation theory at the regional scale.

There are major objections to this view. The first is that although the two sectors may be different at their extremes, they are in reality very closely linked. For example, much of the furniture made in small shanty workshops is sold in large and modern city centre stores. Components made in small workshops may later be included in the assembly of final products made in a large capital intensive factory. Figure 1.20b gives some impression of the linkage of the industrial, retail, wholesale, transport and service components of the formal and informal sectors of the urban economy.

Some writers argue that these links work to the advantage of the formal sector and that low wages and meagre profits result in the informal sector. They also argue that the formal sector raises demand for goods made overseas thereby increasing modern forms of dependency, and depressing further local industry and production. This argument too can be linked to dependency theory at the national and international levels.

Like informal squatter and shanty housing, informal sector jobs make up such a large part of the economy of most Third World cities today that planners and politicians really have no option but to think about them in a positive manner. This was not generally the case in the past. In places where there are so many problems, politicians and planners must take the hopes, desires and abilities of the population into account. In other words, members of the public must be allowed to *participate* fully in the processes of planning and development. Planning must be about the needs of the local, poor and disadvantaged people. Quite simply, the hopes and desires of the ordinary people are the most important resource available to governments in Third World countries.

small and family run, and make use of local materials and resources along with adapted technology. In contrast, there is the *formal sector* of the economy. This is mainly run by large corporations, is capital intensive, and makes extensive use of imported technology and personnel.

It is, of course, difficult to estimate what proportion of the urban workforce is to be found in the informal sector, but studies in Latin American and some Asian cities suggest that the level may be anywhere between 40 and 70 per cent.

During the 1950s and 1960s, again there was a tendency for people to see the informal sector as a

1 INTRODUCTION

In the first part of this book the issues surrounding the role of cities in the process of development have been examined. In Part II examples of the topics dealt with in Part I are provided. Overall, the focus is on the ways in which governments have responded to the problems surrounding the growth of cities in Third World countries.

The involvement of the government and its agencies in trying to direct how things will develop in the future is referred to as *planning*. In Part II we examine two issues:

1. examples of urbanisation and planning at the *national level*, focusing in particular on the degree to which planning has been *top-down* or *bottom-up*;
2. examples of planning for housing and jobs in Third World cities.

It is possible to put forward a model of patterns of urbanisation under different levels of state intervention. This is shown in Figure 2.1. In overall terms, urbanisation has tended to advance most quickly under free-market or capitalist conditions. Rates of urbanisation have most frequently been reduced in countries where

the state has become increasingly involved in planning the economy and its development.

In the post-1945 period, socialist Third World countries such as Cambodia, Vietnam and China have introduced what amount to *anti-urban policies*. This is not because socialism is against cities as such, but rather because cities are seen as being associated with elite social groups and foreign influences. Some countries, for example South Vietnam between 1975 and 1980, have followed a path of *deurbanisation* (Figure 2.1). A less drastic option is one of *zero urban growth*, where little or no change in urban population is allowed, but the existing level is maintained. China, for example, implemented this type of policy during the period 1958–75. In other circumstances, the state may promote *underurbanisation*. This occurs where urbanisation proceeds, but at a rate which is slower than the growth of employment in industry. But urbanisation does not always occur very slowly and in some socialist countries, and indeed state-controlled mixed economies, intensive urbanisation may be promoted. This might occur after a period of deurbanisation, zero urban growth or underurbanisation (Figure 2.1).

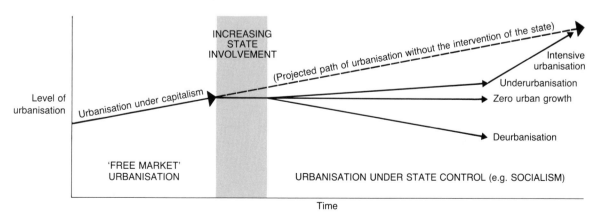

Figure 2.1 *Patterns of urbanisation and state intervention (based on P. Murray and I. Szelenyi, 1984)*

2   URBANISATION AND PLANNING AT THE NATIONAL LEVEL

2.1 Cuba: an example of bottom-up urban planning

Cuba, the largest of the Caribbean islands, was discovered by Columbus in 1492 at the dawn of the Mercantile period. With the exception of a brief spell of British rule in 1762, Spain retained its colonial power over Cuba until defeated in the Spanish-American War of 1898. This represented the start of a period during which the island was dominated by the United States of America, first militarily, and then economically, after independence in 1902.

During the first half of the twentieth century, the country was governed by a series of dictators, the last one being Fulgencio Batista whose corrupt regime had ruled the country from 1933. After a two-year guerilla campaign, a law student, Fidel Castro, and his followers ousted Batista from power in 1959. It is generally accepted that the leaders of the revolution were not initially communists, but fervent nationalists who were opposed to the corruption and inequalities that had existed before. But the antagonistic stance taken by the United States after the revolution resulted in the Cubans increasingly turning to the Soviet Union.

Before the revolution, Havana, the capital, was a classic primate city (Figure 2.2). Most of the wealth and activities of the country were concentrated there. However, it was also characterised by shanty towns, poverty, gambling and vice. By 1953, the Greater Havana area had grown to 1.2 million people, containing 21 per cent of the country's total population. At this time 75 per cent of all industry was found in Havana and 80 per cent of the nation's exports passed through the port, serving to stress the dependent relation of the country to the United States. Most of the country's health care facilities, schools, colleges and cultural organisations were also situated in and around Havana.

Castro and his followers regarded the city as representing capitalist (American) interests and over-privilege. From around 1963, Havana was increasingly discriminated against. Its physical fabric was left to decay so as to make it less attractive to potential rural migrants. Two key

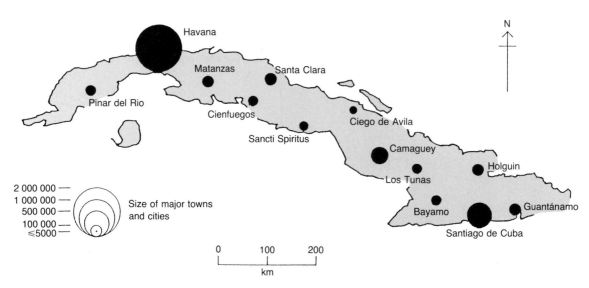

Figure 2.2 *The principal towns of Cuba in 1985*

policies were adopted: the decentralisation of people and activities from Havana; and the reduction of the striking differences which had come to exist between the urban and rural areas of the nation.

Thus, since 1959, promoting a more even geographical pattern of development has been the express aim of the state. The growth of provincial towns in the 20 000 to 200 000 size range has been encouraged. At the next level down, the re-grouping of villages into *rural new towns* (*comunidades*) has occurred. Each rural new town has been developed with its own food and clothing stores, nurseries, primary schools, small clinic, social centre, bookshop and cafes. By 1982 some 360 comunidades had been created. Control has also been exercised over migration, with Ministerial permission being required in order to move to a job in Havana.

Most importantly, massive efforts have been made to develop primary, secondary and tertiary health care facilities throughout the country. Treatment at the centres is free. Primary health care is available throughout Cuba, whilst secondary and tertiary facilities are located in towns and cities. With regard to education too, great improvements have been made. In 1971, only seven out of 478 secondary schools were to be found in rural areas; by 1979, this had changed to 533 rural schools out of a total of 1318. All students are expected to work in agriculture at some stage in an effort to reduce elitist attitudes and values.

Today, Havana has nearly reached the 2 million mark and is certainly much larger than Santiago (351 000) and Camaguey (252 000), the second and third largest cities (Figure 2.2). Some 69 per cent of the total population of Cuba is to be found living in urban settlements.

Cuba has done much to reduce the differences between town and country, although those who are critical of the Marxist approach which has been followed suggest that the same could have been achieved without the state apparatus which controls all sectors of the economy. Such critics also argue that much unemployment is disguised, that rural-urban differences still exist and that elite privileges have re-emerged.

Whatever the ultimate judgement there can be no doubting that Cuba's 10 million inhabitants are now highly dependent on external controlling factors. In 1983, for example, total Soviet assistance to Cuba amounted to $US 4100 millions, consisting of $US 1000 millions development aid and $US 3100 millions in trade subsidies. Thus, Cuba has remained a dependent state, even though this is now a socialist rather than a capitalist form of dependency.

2.2 Nigeria: an example of top-down urban planning

Nigeria is the largest nation in Africa and currently has a population of 94 millions. The Portuguese were the first Europeans to visit what is today the Nigerian coast in 1471, and they were followed by visitors from other European countries. British colonial rule dated from 1900.

From the colonial era to the present, policies have tended to be *top-down* or *from above*, and development has been concentrated into a limited number of areas. Planning strategies, since their introduction in 1946, have been essentially market-oriented, concentrating on the production of agricultural crops for export and *import-substitution* industrialisation. Investment and industrial plants have focused on the cities.

Today, the twelve major cities of Nigeria account for nearly 77 per cent of all industrial establishments in the country and 87 per cent of the total industrial employment. However, in 1985, only 23 per cent of the population lived in towns and cities. Of the total employment in manufacturing, 76 per cent is to be found along the coastal belt (Figure 2.3).

The capital, Lagos, which currently has a population nearing 2 millions, accounts for well over 50 per cent of the nation's industrial wages, nearly 60 per cent of its gross output, 49 per cent of all industrial employment and 38 per cent of total industrial plants. Within each of the states making up the country, services and jobs are also strongly concentrated into the state capital. For example, in the north of the country, in Kano state, the Kano metropolitan area contained 71 of the 73 industries that were operating in 1971, and 11 of the 12 banks.

In such circumstances it is perhaps not surprising that rural-to-urban migration has been very strong and the main cities have grown extremely quickly (Table 2.1). For example, during the period 1952–1963, Port Harcourt grew at the exceptional rate of 10.5 per cent per

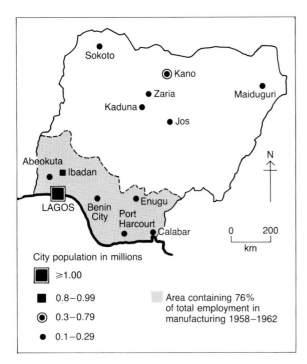

Figure 2.3 *The main cities and principal manufacturing zone of Nigeria (based on M. Filani, 1981)*

Table 2.1 Growth rates of a selection of major Nigerian cities, 1952–1963

City	Population		
	1952	*1963*	*Increase per annum (%)*
Kaduna	42647	129133	10.6
Port Harcourt	59548	179563	10.5
Lagos	267407	665246	8.6
Kano	131316	295432	7.6
Enugu	63212	138457	7.4
Zaria	92434	166170	5.5
Ibadan	406206	635011	3.0

annum, whilst Lagos and Kano increased their populations at 8.6 and 7.6 per cent per annum respectively (Figure 2.4).

A long search for oil proved to be successful in the mid-1950s and by 1963 oil accounted for 3 per cent of government revenues. In 1982, this commodity represented 90 per cent of the value of the country's exports. However, many people maintain that the oil monies have been used inefficiently, leading for example to massive imports of expensive foreign goods.

Whilst many agree that the Nigerian economy has grown, others maintain that it has not developed. They suggest that the majority of the population are not better off and that deep regional inequalities still characterise the country. Such critics state that there have been relatively few trickle-down effects of growth from the urban to rural areas. Too much emphasis has been placed on *sectoral growth* – the promotion of different areas of the economy, such as industry – but little regard has been paid to the geographical consequences. Agriculture has been neglected, the drift from the land to the cities has not been reduced and the country remains strongly dependent on the nations of the West.

Figure 2.4 *Part of the old city of Kano, Nigeria*

3   PLANNING FOR HOUSING AND JOBS IN THIRD WORLD CITIES

3.1 The government must not build houses

Apart from a few wealthy countries, most Third World governments just cannot afford high-rise monumental responses to their housing problems. More to the point, the people who are in urgent need of housing cannot afford them. This has led to what at first sounds like a curious argument — that where there is a housing shortage, the last thing that Third World governments should do is to build houses. Instead, the government should assist the people in their efforts to help themselves.

Over the past ten or so years, the principal international aid agencies, such as the *World Bank* and the *United States Agency for International Aid (USAID)*, who provide Third World governments with loans for housing schemes, have come to support strongly such approaches. Well over thirty Third World countries are now implementing housing projects of this kind. In this way, *spontaneous self-help housing* by the people themselves has given rise to *aided self-help housing* or *ASH* as a major planning policy.

Figure 2.5 shows there are three types of aided self-help housing, although each is closely related. These consist of the (i) *upgrading or improvement of existing squatter settlements and shanty towns*, (ii) the provision of *site and services* and (iii) *core housing* schemes. All three approaches have in common the aim of taking up and encouraging the efforts that ordinary people are making to build houses for themselves. In the next three sections, these approaches are considered in detail. Their chief characteristics are summarised and examples of their implementation provided.

3.2 Aided self-help housing (ASH)

i) Upgrading existing squatter settlements

This is the simplest and most straightforward form of aided self-help where efforts are made to improve the houses and the facilities in an area. The big advantage is that many of the existing houses and jobs are preserved. The retention of the community spirit which has evolved is another important merit of the approach. Upgrading potentially involves three things.

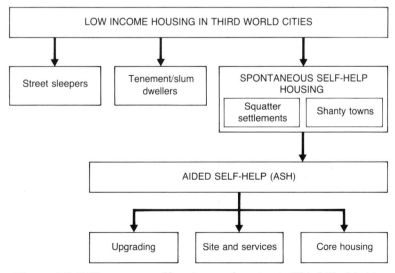

Figure 2.5 *Different types of low-income housing in Third World cities*

First, the provision of the basic services which are missing; for example, water, toilets, electricity, schools, paths and roads.

Secondly, it is usually necessary to improve the physical layout of the area. This reflects the fact that houses have often been built very close together. A typical example is shown in Figure 2.6a. In order to improve the situation it is frequently necessary to define lots around the houses. This is shown in Figure 2.6b. In doing this every effort should be made to minimise the disruption involved. But where the houses are poorly laid out, then it is necessary to move and reposition some of them. A few may have to be demolished entirely. The houses affected in these two ways in the example are clearly indicated in Figure 2.6c. Often this process is referred to as *reblocking*.

Thirdly, and most importantly, the establishment of security of tenure is vital if house owners are to improve their homes. Normally, residents are given the opportunity to become the outright owners of their plots, although in some circumstances long-term leases are provided instead.

An excellent example of the process of upgrading is provided by the Tondo Foreshore Development Project in the city of Manila in the Philippines. This has involved an area of 445 acres of reclaimed land adjacent to the port waterfront area. Over 27 000 families lived here as squatters. The project commenced in 1976 at an estimated total cost of $US 65 millions, approximately half of which was provided by a loan from the World Bank. The three approaches listed above were implemented and, in all, approximately 12 000 houses were upgraded. As a result of reblocking it was necessary for around 4000 families to be moved to new houses. An evaluation survey carried out five years after the start of the project revealed that 97.5 per cent of all households had improved their dwellings and 12.5 per cent had built entirely new ones.

A somewhat different example is provided by Barbados in the eastern part of the Caribbean. Approximately one-third of all families live in small wooden houses which can be moved (see Figure 2.7). These are known as *chattel houses* and they have been built on rented plots by people who work for the sugar plantations. Groups of these houses are known as *tenantries*. When workers leave their jobs, they can take their houses down and move them to a new site. This system reflected the insecurity of tenure which plantation workers faced, but it meant that few people improved their houses substantially. In 1980, two acts were passed. The first gave tenants the right to purchase the land on which their houses were located. The second allowed for general improvements to be made to the tenantries. Jointly, it is hoped these two measures will lead to the rapid upgrading and improving of these areas which have remained largely unchanged for decades.

ii) Site and service schemes

These involve the use of new land which is divided into plots or *sites* on which houses can be built. The plots are then supplied with the basic *services* required by the residents.

In the purest form, therefore, the people are left to build their own houses. This approach retains the advantages of allowing people to build the homes that they can afford and to extend and improve them later as their fortunes improve and their family circumstances change. Sometimes the government may provide technical assistance in the form of advice on building procedures. At the same time, access roads, water, electricity and other essential services, which are invariably missing in squatter settlements and shanty towns, are provided at the outset.

As site and service schemes involve opening up new lands, they are very often constructed on the outskirts of the city where land is relatively cheap. If residents are being moved from squatter settlements that are located nearer to the city centre, then there is often the problem that people are taken away from their places of work. There have even been instances where projects of this type have had to be abandoned as a result of people being separated from their places of employment and/or not being provided with suitable premises for continuing their informal sector activities.

Ensuring that people can continue to earn a living is vital to the success of such schemes. It is a good idea for small premises to be provided so that cottage-type informal sector workshops can be established. As well as this, the provision of security of tenure on the land is vital if the consolidation process is to lead to the gradual improvement of housing in such schemes.

a) Existing unpaved roads   Unpaved and ill-defined paths between houses

b) Roads paved   Lots defined around houses with the minimum movement of structures

c)

Houses retained

Houses repositioned on existing lot

Houses demolished

0   50
Metres

Figure 2.6 *An example of a squatter upgrading scheme (based on A. Turner, 1980)*

An example of the putting into practice of the approach is afforded by the Dandora project in Nairobi, the capital city of Kenya. This is a large-scale attempt by the Nairobi City Council together with the Government of Kenya to provide low-cost housing. The aim is to provide as many as 6000 serviced plots for building over a seven-year period. Each plot will be between 100 and 160 square metres in area and will be provided with individual water and sewerage connections, access roads, lighting and refuse disposal facilities. Once again the World Bank, along with the International Bank for Reconstruction and Development (IBRD) and the International Development Agency (IDA), has provided funding.

iii) Core housing schemes

There is a form of site and service housing which involves the provision of the first stages of the house. Sometimes this merely involves the building of a small unit containing a toilet and bathroom. This initial section of the dwelling is called a *core unit*. If this comprises only a toilet and bathroom it is referred to as a *wet core*.

One of the main advantages of core housing is that it helps to ensure that health and sanitary conditions are much better than those found in the majority of squatter settlements and shanty towns. Another merit is its flexibility. The core unit can extend from the provision of a toilet and bathroom, to a toilet and bathroom plus a brick-built wall, to all those plus a kitchen and a finished room, or indeed even the shell of the entire house. Often a mixture of different types of unit is provided within a new core housing area.

An example of the proposed use of the core housing principle is shown in Figure 2.7 in the case of Barbados. In the previous section the moveable chattel houses of Barbados were described. In the first diagram, shown at the top of Figure 2.7, provision is made for the placing of a traditional self-built chattel house on a site with a wet core and kitchen unit (Figure 2.7a). In Figure 2.7b, the process is taken a stage further and the same type of wet core is provided as an in-built part of a relatively simple *starter house* which has been constructed of brick. This suggests the variations possible on a site and service scheme, extending from the inclusion of traditional house types for relatively poor people,

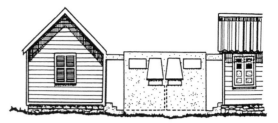

a) Twin core with chattel house

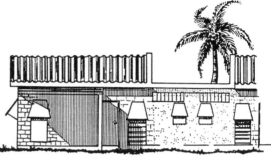

b) Connected starter houses

Figure 2.7 *The drawings show proposals for a core housing scheme and a starter house in Barbados in the Caribbean. The photo shows a traditional Barbadian chattel house*

through to the provision of basic houses in permanent materials for those who can afford to pay for them.

The fact that such housing developments should be *affordable* to the people for whom they are planned, and that the costs of constructing them should be *recovered* by the government, is increasingly recognised as being of fundamental importance if site and service and core housing schemes are to be successful in meeting their long term aims.

3.3 Planning for jobs and prosperity

The need to ensure that housing schemes do not serve to separate low-income families from their jobs and workshops has been stressed in the previous sections. The provision of suitable units which can be used as small workshops is a vital component of successful schemes.

A good example is afforded in the case of Delhi, the capital city of India. Here, a planned industrial township is currently being established in an effort to house small industries of the informal sector which were previously operating in an unauthorised and illegal manner in unsuitable areas of the city. This development is

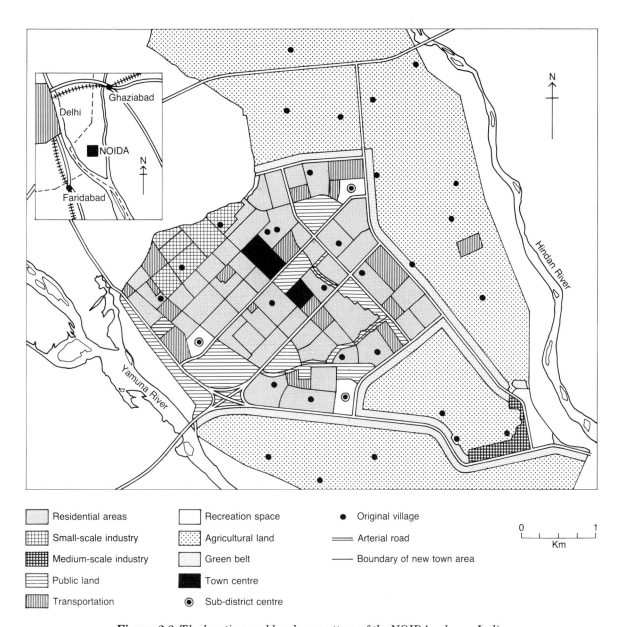

Residential areas

Small-scale industry

Medium-scale industry

Public land

Transportation

Recreation space

Agricultural land

Green belt

Town centre

Sub-district centre

● Original village

═══ Arterial road

─── Boundary of new town area

0   1
Km

Figure 2.8 *The location and land use pattern of the NOIDA scheme, India*

known as NOIDA (the New Okhla Industrial Development Area). The industrial township is located twelve kilometres south-east from the centre of Delhi. It is being designed to house about 5000 small-scale industrial units along with housing for the workers. The overall structure of NOIDA is illustrated in Figure 2.8.

It must be emphasised in any consideration of planning for housing and jobs in Third World cities that the poor residential conditions and high rates of unemployment reflect the poverty which characterises society as a whole. These conditions are not ones which are somehow created by urban areas themselves. They reflect the uneven distribution of wealth that occurs within societies as a whole. Thus, if meaningful progress is to be made, broad political action is required. It is not just a question of providing more jobs or more new houses.

Frequently, major reforms are required to the structure of society. For example, in most countries the main problem with housing is the lack of access that the majority of ordinary people have to land. Land prices are so high as to make ownership impossible for the poor. Increasingly, the supply of land is so restricted that squatting is becoming very difficult, if not impossible. The state, the church, the military and rich families, including politicians, often own vast tracts of land, sometimes purely for reasons of speculation. At the very least, government schemes of *land banking* and *pooling* are required whereby land can be collected together and then made available to those who are in most need of it.

Without a genuine willingness to improve the lot of both the urban poor and the rural poor in Third World countries, it seems that many countless millions are destined to live lives of abject poverty. This is despite the manifest efforts that the majority are making to improve the conditions under which they find themselves.

1 MONITORING THIRD WORLD URBAN DEVELOPMENT

1.1 Data sources

The past forty-year period has seen the most rapid rate of world urbanisation ever known. This has been due to the very rapid rate of urban growth that has occurred in the Third World. In each of the decades of the 1960s and the 1970s, the urban population of the world increased by almost 17 per cent. If this rate of urban change had continued unaltered, the world would have been totally urbanised by the year 2031. Clearly, this rate had to diminish somewhat, although it is still expected that global urbanisation will reach the 90 per cent level by the year 2060.

There are a number of important statistical sources that can be consulted by those who are interested in what is happening to the towns and cities of the world and to levels of urbanisation. There are three sources which are generally available. These can be consulted in most libraries by those who wish to monitor the process of urban development in the Third World.

World Development Report: This has been published annually for the World Bank by Oxford University Press since 1978. Its aim is to assess the key development issues which the world faces. Reports contain statistics on vital urban indicators for countries and groups of countries. These include: overall levels of urbanisation, average annual growth rates of urban population, the proportion of the total population of nations living in the largest city and in cities of over 500 000, and the number of cities with more than 500 000 inhabitants. In addition, for those wishing to compare aspects of urbanisation with basic indicators of economic development, levels of *Gross Domestic Product per capita* are listed for countries.

Demographic Yearbook: The United Nations Department of International Economic and Social Affairs publishes this basic guide to demographic data. Issues contain regular listings of the population of all world cities with over 100 000 inhabitants, plus capital cities which are smaller than this.

The Geographical Digest: This most useful guide has been published on an annual basis by George Philip for over twenty years. In 1986, it appeared in a new larger format and was scheduled for publication on a periodic basis. The 1986 edition lists, for most world countries, the percentage of the population that was urban in 1950 and 1985. It also includes the population size of the world's principal cities – those with 100 000 or more inhabitants.

1.2 Using newspapers and magazines

Another simple but most effective method of monitoring the progress of Third World urbanisation is by means of regularly scanning the foreign sections of major international newspapers and magazines. These very often contain detailed reports of major events such as the riots over food prices that occurred in Caracas, Venezuela, in 1988, the destruction of homes by natural disasters such as Hurricane Gilbert and Hurricane Hugo in the Caribbean in 1988 and 1989 respectively, or by flooding, as in the case of Khartoum, Sudan, in 1988. Smaller scale events, such as rains causing heavy landslides in squatter settlements, are also frequently described.

Collecting and categorising reports on such events over a given period of time can provide useful information on Third World cities and the pressing development problems they face.

(i)   Examine a selection of newspapers and magazines of your choice over a period of one, or perhaps three months.

(ii) Cut out any reports and articles which describe conditions in Third World cities.

(iii) For each report or article, pinpoint the location of the city on an outline map of the world.

(iv) Draw up a table with the following headings:

a) size of city; b) capital city or not; c) country; d) continent; e) type of event (for example, flood, riot, mudslide); f) scale of the event (for example, number of people involved). Enter full details of each event under these headings.

(v) What do your results suggest are the main problems facing Third World cities? Do these problems vary from place to place?

2   URBAN GROWTH RATE AND LEVELS OF DEVELOPMENT

At the beginning of this book, it was stressed how it is in the poorer countries of the world that cities are today growing most rapidly. This exercise employs data taken from the sources listed in the previous section in order to examine this relationship in detail.

Two sets of data have been taken from the *World Development Report* for a selection of low-, middle- and high-income countries. The first is the annual growth of urban population per annum during the decade 1970–1980. The second variable shows what is known as the *Gross Domestic Product (US dollars) per capita* (GDP per capita) of these countries.

Levels of GDP per capita are often used as a broad measure of the level of economic development that has been attained by a country. The *Gross Domestic Product* is the total value of all the commodities produced in the country. If this total is divided by the population, then this is referred to as the *GDP per capita*.

For the data listed for the 33 countries in Table 3.1:

(i)   Calculate the mean annual percentage urban growth rate for each of the three groups of countries. Which group has the *highest* rate of growth?

(ii) Calculate the mean level of GDP per capita for the three groups of countries. Which group has the *lowest* level of GDP per capita?

(iii) a) Draw a scattergraph showing the relationship between urban growth rates and levels of GDP for the 33 countries listed. On the graph label the horizontal axis (x)

'GDP per capita' and the vertical axis (y) 'Rates of urban growth'.

b) What does the scattergraph suggest about the relationship?

(iv) a) Rank each of the data sets from high to low values (1 = high to 33 = low).

b) Using the Spearman's rank correlation coefficient technique, calculate the level of correlation existing between rates of urban growth and levels of GDP per capita.

Spearman's rank (r_s) is calculated according to the formula:

$$r_s = 1 - \left(\frac{6 \sum d^2}{N^3 - N} \right)$$

where d = the difference between the rankings

N = the number of observations

c) Test for significance using the Students t test:

$$t = r_s \sqrt{\frac{N - 2}{1 - r_s^2}}$$

d) Comment briefly on the broad relationship which exists between the two variables.

(v) a) On the scattergraph, draw in the overall trend or best-fit line, by eye.

b) Which countries deviate most from this best-fit line?

c) Suggest reasons why some countries do not follow the overall trend.

Table 3.1 Urban growth rates and Gross Domestic Product per capita for a selection of low-, medium- and high-income countries

Country	Urban growth per annum (%) 1970–1980	GDP per capita $US 1979	Country	Urban growth per annum (%) 1970–1980	GDP per capita $US 1979
A. LOW-INCOME COUNTRIES			**C. HIGH-INCOME COUNTRIES**		
Bangladesh	6.8	90	Italy	1.3	5,250
Nepal	4.7	130	United Kingdom	0.3	6,320
Burma	3.9	160	Finland	2.7	8,160
Burundi	2.5	180	Japan	2.0	8,810
Malawi	6.8	200	France	1.4	9,950
Benin	3.9	250	Netherlands	0.6	10,230
China	3.1	260	United States	1.5	10,630
Tanzania	8.7	260	Belgium	0.4	10,920
Guinea	5.5	280	Denmark	0.9	11,900
Uganda	7.0	290	Sweden	1.0	11,930
Togo	5.6	350	Switzerland	1.0	13,920
B. MEDIUM-INCOME COUNTRIES					
Kenya	6.8	380			
Senegal	3.3	430			
Honduras	5.5	530			
Philippines	3.6	600			
El Salvador	3.3	670			
Mongolia	4.1	780			
Colombia	3.9	1,010			
Ivory Coast	8.5	1,040			
Panama	3.6	1,400			
Brazil	3.7	1,780			
Trinidad and Tobago	1.3	3,390			

3   HOUSING CONDITIONS IN A CARIBBEAN CITY

The housing system of Barbados was briefly discussed in Part II. It was noted that, due to insecurity of land tenure, traditional houses have been built in a manner which allows them to be moved as and when the need arises.

Such dwellings are referred to as *chattel houses* (see Figure 2.7). These are constructed of wood and are set on a pile of rocks. Such dwellings do not have water-borne toilets, but make use of pit latrines, where a pit or hole is bored into the rock. In the past, many such homes did not have an electricity supply.

Bridgetown is the capital of Barbados. Approximately 100 000 people or 42 per cent of the total population is to be found living in the wider metropolitan area. In every respect, Bridgetown is a bustling, busy and congested primate city.

Three key housing variables are listed in Table 3.2 for the nine major divisions which make up the Greater Metropolitan area of Barbados. A base map showing these areas is provided in Figure 3.1. The variables cover three aspects of housing conditions which relate to chattel-style dwellings.

(i)   For each variable draw a choropleth map to show variations in percentage scores. Use a different shading for every ten per cent difference in values.

Table 3.2 Key housing characteristics for the principal sub-areas making up Bridgetown, Barbados

		Percentage of houses:		
Area	Key on map	Constructed entirely of wood	Using pit latrine	Supplied with electriticity
Bridgetown	City	73.19	61.81	76.18
West		44.98	37.89	89.48
North-East		51.29	45.33	86.70
Central North		68.88	59.31	82.19
Central East		71.05	64.63	83.65
Central West		59.79	52.35	84.47
Central South		54.01	47.90	88.30
East		41.18	36.77	88.91
Christ Church West		41.70	33.22	90.43

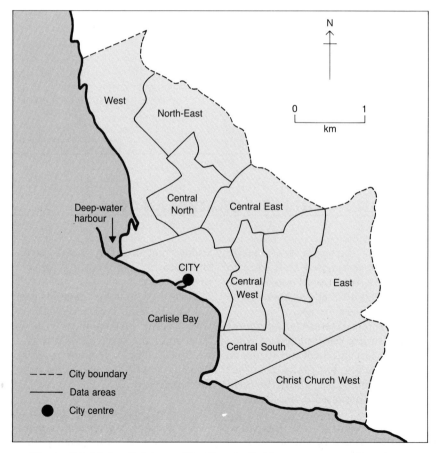

Figure 3.1 *Major divisions of the Greater Bridgetown metropolitan area*

(ii)   Do the patterns suggest any similarity to the standard models of urban structure? Compare the pattern with those shown in Figure 1.12.

(iii) a) Rank each of the data sets from high to low values (1 = high to 9 = low).

b) Using Spearman's rank correlation co-efficient, calculate the correlations existing between these variables. Three correlation coefficients are to be calculated. Once calculated they can be placed in a simple correlation matrix, as shown here:

	wood	pit latrine	electricity
wood	1.00	–	–
pit latrine		1.00	–
electricity			1.00

c) Comment on the relationships existing between the three variables.

(iv) Considering both the patterns and correlation scores for Bridgetown, what can be said about the nature of poor housing conditions in Third World cities?

4   UPGRADING AN UNPLANNED HOUSING AREA

An unplanned housing area is shown in Figure 3.2. This is the Conway district as it existed in 1983. It is located near to the harbour in Castries, the capital of the Caribbean island of St Lucia. The Conway area was characterised by an unplanned scattering of wooden dwellings and workshops. But the surrounding area was underdeveloped except for the St Lucia Port Authority warehouse which occupied a prime location adjacent to the John Compton Highway.

Figure 3.3 shows a view across part of the area. The photograph was taken from the point marked with the letter 'V' on Figure 3.2. This is located on a bluff of higher land which exists to the west of the low-income area. Figure 3.3 shows clearly the types of houses that the area contains and the degree of crowding.

(i)   Comment on the location of the Conway housing area in relation to the types of land use which are to be found surrounding it.

(ii)   Suggest the types of jobs that the residents of the Conway area are likely to carry out.

(iii) For some years now it has been planned that the entire Conway area, the land within the heavy dotted line on Figure 3.2, should be redeveloped. In fact, since 1986, a part of the area has been cleared and rebuilt – but only a part of it.

a) Your task is to prepare a development plan for the whole of the Conway area. Different groups will often have very different ideas as to what should go ahead. For this exercise three groups representing different interests have been identified: people living in the area; planners; politicians.

Bear in mind that people living in the area will probably wish to stay there and improve their homes. They may well work in the area or very nearby. The planners on the other hand will want to reduce crowding and improve services. The politicians wish to see the area looking more modern, although the cost involved in achieving this is very important to them.

b) For each role, make a list of the main things that you consider need to be done in order to improve the area.

c) For each role, which of these things need to be done first? Place the entire list of things to be done in order of priority.

d) For each role, draw a sketch showing your plan for the area.

e) If the exercise is being carried out by small groups you can develop the role play further. Appoint a chairperson. This person should assume the role of being the island's Prime Minister.

The three different groups should draw up their plans for the improvement of the area separately. When they have done so, they should meet together and examine the degree to which they are in agreement as to how the area should be upgraded and redeveloped. This meeting will be chaired by the Prime Minister. Make a note of how decisions are reached. Was each group satisfied with the final outcome?

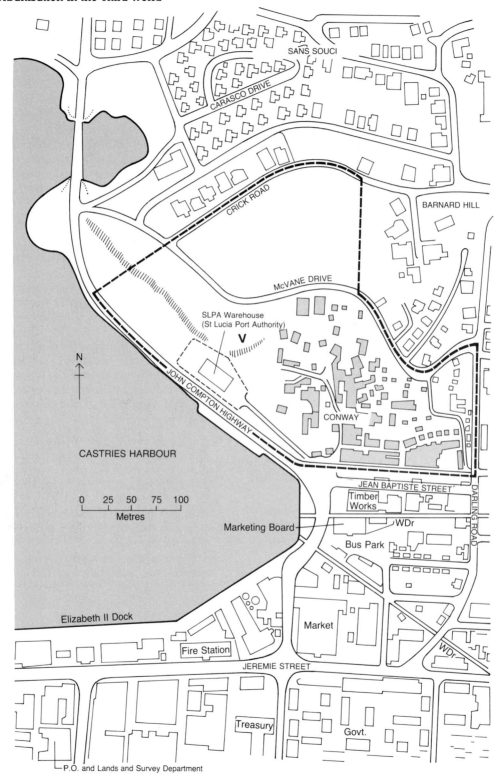

SANS SOUCI

CARASCO DRIVE

CRICK ROAD

BARNARD HILL

McVANE DRIVE

SLPA Warehouse
(St Lucia Port Authority)

V

N

JOHN COMPTON HIGHWAY

CONWAY

CASTRIES HARBOUR

0   25   50   75   100
Metres

JEAN BAPTISTE STREET

DARLING ROAD

Timber
Works

Marketing Board

WDr

Bus Park

Elizabeth II Dock

Market

Fire Station

WDr

JEREMIE STREET

Treasury

Govt.

P.O. and Lands and Survey Department

◄ **Figure 3.2** *The Conway area of Castries, St Lucia*

Figure 3.3 *A view over the Conway area, Castries, St Lucia, taken from the point marked 'V' on the map in Figure 3.2*

SUGGESTED READING

Armstrong, W. and McGee, T.G. (1985): *Theatres of Accumulation: Studies in Asian and Latin American Urbanization*, London and New York: Methuen

Forbes, D. and Thrift, N. (1987) (eds): *The Socialist Third World; Urban Development and Territorial Planning*, Oxford: Blackwell

Gilbert, A. G. and Gugler, J. (1982): *Cities, Poverty and Development: Urbanisation in the Third World*, London and Oxford: Oxford University Press

Lloyd, P. (1979): *Slums of Hope?: Shanty Towns of the Third World*, Harmondsworth: Penguin

Payne, G. K. (ed) (1984): *Low-income Housing in the Developing World: The role of sites and services and settlement upgrading*, Chichester: Wiley

Potter, R. B. (1985): *Urbanisation and Planning in the Third World: Spatial Perceptions and Public Participation*, London and Sydney: Croom Helm

Potter, R. B. and Unwin, T. (1989) (eds): *The Geography of Urban-Rural Interaction in Developing Countries*, London and New York: Routledge

Potter, R. B. (1989): (ed) *Urbanization, Planning and Development in the Caribbean*, London and New York: Mansell

Skinner, R. J. and Rodell, M. J. (eds) (1983): *People, Poverty and Shelter: Problems of self-help housing in the Third World*, London: Methuen

Stöhr, W. B. and Taylor, D. R.F. (eds) (1981): *Development form Above or Below?: The dialectics of Regional Planning in Developing Countries*, Chichester: Wiley

INDEX